CHANGED

Mission Trip Devotions & Journal

LENA WOOD

Standard
PUBLISHING
Bringing The Word to Life
Cincinnati, Ohio

Published by Standard Publishing, Cincinnati, Ohio

www.standardpub.com

Project editor: Lynn Lusby Pratt

Cover and interior design: The DesignWorks Group

Printed in: China

ISBN 978-0-7847-2286-2

14 13 12 11 10 09 08   9 8 7 6 5 4 3 2 1

TRACKING THE CHANGES

There's a cool editorial tool you may have on your computer. It's called "track changes." With this little tool, an editor can highlight in a bright color the revisions she's made on a manuscript so the writer and editor may easily track them.

In much the same way, the purpose of this journal is to help you track the changes to your life and spirit as a result of the mission trip. We'll highlight reverse culture shock, getting perspective from a distance, relating to relatives, and sampling a few creative ministries worldwide that you may never have heard of. Not to mention the perennial, post-mission question: "Where do I go from here?"

If you've been deeply affected—changed—by your mission experience, you'll enjoy these debriefing devos, reliving the highlights. As normal life sets back in, it's way too easy to lose the precious details of your adventure.

Here's what you get in each of the fifteen devotions:

- A thought-provoking meditation with Scriptures and extra helps on prayer, travel, or culture
- Lined journal pages for writing your thoughts and prayers
- A blank page for sketching, or as a mini-scrapbook page for pictures, stamps, addresses, ticket stubs, and other mementos you find in the bottom of your luggage!

You'll continue to enrich your mission experience by savoring the memories and learning from them. Let the Lord teach you on a deeper level. Jesus told his disciples, "I tell you the truth, unless you change and become like little children, you will never enter the kingdom of heaven. Therefore, whoever humbles himself like this child is the greatest in the kingdom of heaven" (Matthew 18:3, 4).

We can all use a little retooling.

If your trip was brief—ten days or less—you may not feel the full force of reverse culture shock. But long trip or short, you're back. And though you generally look like the same person, deep inside you've *changed*.

LOST IN SPACE

Unless you've stopped for official debriefing with a mission sending agency, you're home. Who knows what kind of shape you're in! Bring any tropical diseases, foot fungi, or other battle scars home with you? Is your mind elsewhere? Does your heart need a little TLC?

Spiritually inspired emotions can run very deep. Don't underestimate them or dismiss them.

My daughter Arian's first mission trip was to Seattle, a Campus Crusade summer project, working with foreign college students. My niece was living in Seattle at the time, so the fam decided to fly out from Ohio at the end of the summer to visit my niece and bring my daughter home. Instead of flying back, we opted for a post-mission adventure for Arian, and a long-held dream for the rest of us: driving across the Great Northwest. For five freewheeling days we hit the high spots, traversing mountain ranges, enjoying spacious skies and waves of grain, switching drivers often to keep moving. A road trip on steroids!

But Arian spent most of the time curled up in the back seat of the van with her blanket and pillow. We'd wake her up to marvel at a mountain or take nourishment. I was a little irritated that she wasn't gung ho like the rest of us. My sister jokingly called her "the preemie," since she was mostly eating and sleeping.

We should have known what was going on; we'd simply forgotten what it's like that first time when the Lord opens your eyes and breaks your heart. It had been decades since I'd been a college student on mission for the first time . . . feeling ripped in two as I waved good-bye to return home.

It can be pretty overwhelming. Those last all-nighters, the new friends on the brink of eternal decisions. Decisions they'd make because of—or in spite of—what you said. Friends you may never see again.

I was insensitive to my daughter, and I now apologize before God and all creation!

Learn from my mistake. You or others on your team may be in a mental fog or in emotional pain. You may wake up one morning wondering where you are, strangely homesick for the place you left. Even seasoned ministers have been overwhelmed when the Lord sets them afire with a new direction for their lives.

Conversely, if you're the pragmatic, mission-accomplished type, you're already looking ahead, updating e-mails, jotting notes on your calendar. Others may interpret your attitude as uncaring. And as for your family's response, you may need to skip ahead to the devo on page 27 about parents of missionaries . . . or possibly the one on page 145, "Living Among Pagans"!

At any rate . . . breathe in, breathe out. It's pamper time. As you settle in, consider the reactions of team members and the host missionary when you parted ways. If you're too busy now to make notes about them, draw emoticons of their various expressions: simple smiley, frowny, or weepy faces with a name below each one.

Giving Thanks

How many of these adjectives describe you? Circle all that apply: bone-tired, brokenhearted, gratified, disillusioned, torn, energized, chewed up and spit out, ill, numb, exhilarated, stunned, blissful.

PRAYER

Now pause to focus on praise and gratitude. Even if your trip was a bummer, you can still be thankful.

For one, you didn't have to serve in Death Valley, Chernobyl, Manchac Swamp, or other Worst Places in the World like Centralia, Pennsylvania—a town permanently shut down due to fire and brimstone.

Secondly, you were called to mission for God's purpose—even if the experience was less than exhilarating. Think back to Jonah's mission trip: bad for him, good for Nineveh.

As you unpack and do laundry, thank God for visible blessings: those souvenirs you packed into your bags as tight as the stones of the Great Pyramids. And photos. Thank God that we can capture moments in color to share with church and family. Thank him for technology, which made your trip faster and easier than those trips taken by the pilgrims of old. Did you miss your appliances? clean and hot water? a flushing commode? You got 'em back!

Missions is about people. Pray for your team, your host, new friends. Thank God for your enemies—if you made any. Enemies make great teachers.

Your money and energy may be spent, but the gratitude goes on. Don't forget to re-thank your supporters. Their generosity got you there and back.

Thank your Savior for salvation. Do you view eternity with renewed appreciation and perspective?

If you feel like writing—no pressure here—jot down some special experiences to elaborate on later, particularly ones you might forget.

Debriefing

Circle any of these ministry roles you filled, however briefly: disciple maker, Bible teacher, prayer warrior, relationship builder, healer, exorcist, planner, helper, preacher, baptizer, church planter, maid, builder, educator, painter, worship leader, mechanic, babysitter, cook, counselor, rescuer.

Were any of these roles a surprise?

Tonight watch the sunset, stroll in the moonlight, or listen to the rain. Fall asleep with gratitude in your heart, not just for the past season of your life, but for what lies ahead. Be quiet . . .

"Like cold water to a weary soul is good news from a distant land" (Proverbs 25:25).

"Come to me, all you who are weary and burdened, and I will give you rest. Take my yoke upon you and learn from me, for I am gentle and humble in heart, and you will find rest for your souls. For my yoke is easy and my burden is light" (Matthew 11:28, 29).

EXTREME TOP TEN

If you read the earlier books in this series, you may recall the phrase, "He endured what he hated to achieve what he loved." That certainly describes Jesus enduring the despised cross to achieve the salvation of those he loves. It was his eternal mission, and he endured extremes to accomplish it.

Your mission—as all missions do—most certainly had a few extremes, good and bad: things you loved and things you didn't. It's the extremes that qualify a short-term trip as an adventure. Here's a chance to reflect on your top tens. If your team plans a debriefing time, this would be a fun thing to share.

Sprinkled throughout the list are representative samples from around the world.

1. Most prized souvenir

Mine was the walking stick I used to climb Mt. Fuji.

2. Food extremes—best and worst

(Did anyone out there have the grilled tarantula? I hear it tastes like chicken.)

3. Worst Faux Pas

CULTURE

Here's one from Asia:

I was talking with my church friends during the Sunday school hour, sharing some insight I'd learned from an English language book titled *Cat and Dog Theology*—basically that we shouldn't be like cats (self-righteous, haughty, aloof) but more like dogs (loyal, adoring, serving) in our relationship with God. I didn't know the "be like a dog" metaphor was completely inappropriate. This culture thinks of dogs as very low animals! A few weeks later, the pastor asked me to share something with the congregation, but tactfully advised me, "Just don't talk about being like dogs." I was so mortified!

(You mean in some cultures all dogs don't go to Heaven?!)

4. Best Scenery

From a globe trekker who's been to England, Ireland, France, Thailand, Japan, Laos, Canada, Nepal, England, Taiwan, Myanmar, and Turkey: "Undeniably the Himalayas. Pristine, giant, gorgeous mountains! One interesting detail, however . . .

it almost seemed to me that these mountains had personality, and that they were overly proud of themselves. Perhaps the spirits or principalities that dwell there . . ."

5. Favorite Natural Resource

Was it the natural hot springs baths? the home-grown coffee beans? amazing wild animals? clear night skies? jungle flora and fauna? exotic spices? unique building materials? edible plants? Find a special resource given by God to this specific area. If you worked in the inner city or in a war zone, the greatest natural resource might be the resilience of the local people.

6. Favorite Bible Verse

My favorite is the one I pray at the "gateways to the gods," reclaiming pagan territory for the Lord: "This is the gate of the LORD through which the righteous may enter. . . . Lift up your heads, O you gates; be lifted up, you ancient doors, that the King of glory may come in. Who is this King of glory? The LORD strong and mighty, the LORD mighty in battle. . . . He is the King of glory" (Psalm 118:20; 24:7-10).

7. Most Culture-y Moment

These are epiphany moments when you realize you are *so* in another culture! You're driving along the Irish countryside, thinking how Missouri-like it looks when there in a meadow sits a huge, medieval castle! Or you have to take a bath while partially clothed, under a water barrel shower—outdoors—as a water buffalo approaches and a little boy rides his tricycle past. You're not in Kansas anymore; you're in the hill country of Thailand. Or you get the sampler platter

at a restaurant and everything on it is fried! No wait
. . . that can only mean you're in the United States. So
maybe you get the sampler platter and everything still
has heads attached!

8. Favorite Custom

What little customs made you think, *Hmm, nice
idea. We should do that at home?*

On my first flight with China Airlines, passengers
were given hot washcloths to wipe hands and faces
before the meal. A nice, comforting touch that our
family uses on occasion.

9. Scary Moment

Here's one from an American woman in Turkey:

I was walking around Heybeli, an island near Istanbul. I passed by a gate where the guy seemed to indicate that I should pay some money, but there were no signs in English. Some guy approached, paid for me, then proceeded to walk and talk with me into a semi-dark, wooded area. I hardly saw any other people. After I refused to sit at a picnic table and talk with him, he left me alone. After a while I came out of the woods and happened upon a garbage dump inhabited by gypsies. I passed some horses wandering around (this was a car-less island). Toward the end of my perimeter walk (about five miles), I spotted an old Christian-looking relic. I took a picture and was immediately shouted at by a man holding an automatic weapon, "No picture! No picture!" I offered him my camera rather than face charges, but thankfully he let me go, warning me to take no more photos. I was glad to get back on the ferry, but not sure I knew the way back to my friends' flat. Thankfully, I did.

10. Most Inspiring Moment or Person

For me it's the missionary widows—some in their eighties and nineties—who still serve overseas.

It's the extreme moments that expand your worldview, lift you to new heights of fulfillment, test your faith, melt your heart, and encourage you to storm the gates and serve with new intensity.

TRAVEL

If you used a passport on this trip, check the expiration date before you chuck it into a drawer. You should keep it updated . . . in case God calls and says, "Go. Now!" If you don't have a passport, you might want to think about getting one. You never know. . . .

POMS, COMS,
AND OTHER FOMS

There's a kind of celebrity status that comes with being a short-termer. Most likely you or your team will give a presentation at church. This is important. Potential missionaries may be sitting in the audience. How might you influence individuals and your church family for future work?

Your supporters will want to know how their hard-earned dollars were spent—and well they should. So you have at least one more short-term journey: to the stage. Don't wing it. The Lord's work deserves your very best. Present the work in clear, upbeat fashion. Time your talk beforehand.

Unless you're already famous, here's your fifteen minutes of fame! Actually, you may get only three. Use the time to the fullest. Engage the five senses to give your hearers a rich experience. Use music, video, photos, native dress (if applicable), snacks, and information handouts. (If you were working in the 10/40 Window, most blends of Starbucks coffee come from there. If you promise to give them a plug, they might donate a pound.) For the children, have a display of things to touch.

Give a few stats and facts for a quick overview. Talk mostly about what God is doing in that part of the world. Flip back through your journals; share what God has done in your own heart. Include meaningful Scriptures.

TRAVEL

Your trip might present opportunities to travel and speak on behalf of the mission work. Local civic clubs or schools might be interested in cultural aspects of the place you visited. If your work included construction, well-digging, or orphanage care, consider asking local agencies to partner with you financially, especially if you plan on going again. See if the local newspaper will run a story.

Telling Your Story at Home

If you're not doing a presentation at your home church, you'll still be telling your family. Occasionally the short-termer returns fired up to tell his stories, and then gets mixed reviews. If that happens, don't take it personally. As much as they love you, they may not relate to what you've been through. Remember to listen with genuine interest to what's been going on at home.

For a time you could feel less in sync with your family than with your team, particularly if you've had an extended stay on the field or gone through intense situations. Readjustment with the family might take time, especially if they're not believers.

PRAYER

Present your relationships to the Lord today, both those with your mission team members and with your family.

POMs

The National Network of Parents of Missionaries was born when Diane Stortz's daughter was planning to go to Bosnia long term. It was difficult and lonely for Diane; she didn't know where to turn for emotional support. She turned trial into blessing by teaming with Cheryl Savageau to form a national network devoted to bringing parents of Christian missionaries together. Diane and Cheryl have created a Web site, www.pomnet.org, and a book: *Parents of Missionaries: How to Thrive and Stay Connected When Your Children and Grandchildren Serve Cross-Culturally*. Young adults bitten by the mission bug can get their parents connected. Think of linking with mission projects from all over the world!

Missions changes everyone in the family, those at home and those who go. Diane saw this on her daughter's first furlough. Shiela used to love going to the mall, but now after a brief time shopping, she said, "OK, Mom, that's it. Let's go home." Accustomed to smaller stores and simpler selection in her host country, Sheila was overwhelmed—and disturbed—by the abundance. (You might have felt this way too.)

Conversely, Diane recalled her first visit to Sheila's new home in Bosnia. "My son-in-law pulled the car into a gravel parking lot. I surveyed the lawn of dirt and weeds and the apartment building covered with graffiti, and I stifled an inward cry: *This is where they LIVE?!* We climbed the dusty cement stairwell to the fifth floor and stepped into a sparkling, comfortable apartment. Then I realized that my daughter and her husband were thriving and happy with their life for God in this 'strange' place."

If you're a young adult now considering full-time work, urge your parents to visit you on the field. They'll be amazed at how the world shrinks once they've walked your new turf and met your new friends.

COMs

If you're called to missions later in life, this surprising change can be unsettling, even to your grown children. More retirees are trading their golden years on Golden Pond for a tour of duty across the Big

Pond. Adult children of missionaries (COMs) might experience a sense of abandonment; they may think you've gone a little nuts. *Mom's sporting a bandanna and cargo pants and wearing a backpack?*

FOMs

Friends of missionaries (FOMs) may get a jolt too. One short-termer admitted, "The returnee is still 'feeling' the situation of his field and may be hard on people back here." A long-termer was irritated at stateside Christian publishers: "We have so many choices, but Sunday school material for kids in my field was minimal."

Having seen the horrors of a war-torn country or inner city where people have so little, one can return disillusioned with American wealth and waste, looking critically not only at his own abundance, but at the luxury of friends and neighbors.

You've grasped it by now: we Americans are very rich compared to the rest of the world. Few countries—even those with equal per capita income—have the freedoms, the wide-open spaces, and cheap goods available to us.

Some may interpret your criticisms of the U.S. or your new passion for a different country as sort of unpatriotic. No need to reject one country for another, but to reset priorities.

If any of these scenarios describes you, understand that you're dealing with reverse culture shock. Give yourself and others time to adjust.

For now, "set your mind on things above" (Colossians 3:2). Make notes on what to say in your talk. Use your minutes of fame to inspire and motivate others. Remember how Tom Sawyer got his friends to paint the fence? He seemed so enthused about it, the friends couldn't resist joining him. Your genuine enthusiasm just might spread the light. Go get 'em!

LIVING SACRIFICES

I wonder why some mystics of old felt the need to wear barbed-wire underwear. (I don't think about it often, so don't worry about me.) But the most widely admired ascetics were known to beat themselves bloody, starve themselves, live in desert caves while weaving baskets, chanting, and nibbling old cabbage—for the love of Jesus and to atone for the sins of the world. I wonder about that.

A milder form of self-abuse crops up in our town every spring when devotees crawl up eighty stone steps to a cathedral on a hill. As I watch these good folks on the local news praying, grimacing, and bloodying their knees, I wonder, *Why? Isn't there enough work to do in the world?* Like cleaning a widow's basement or caring for toddlers in the church nursery? Or teaching—there are junior highers in need of love and acceptance.

Isn't real life hard enough? Who needs a spiked girdle?

CULTURE

What was the most grueling work you saw or experienced in the culture you visited? Did you see in the religion there a burdensome theology of works to appease God (or the gods)?

Holy and Pleasing

Paul said, "I urge you, brothers, in view of God's mercy, to offer your bodies as living sacrifices, holy and pleasing to God—this is your spiritual act of worship. Do not conform any longer to the pattern of this world, but be transformed by the renewing of your mind. Then you will be able to test and approve what God's will is—his good, pleasing and perfect will" (Romans 12:1, 2).

The word "offer" here means to hand over, to present. Sacrifices in the Old Testament were presented as substitute atonements for sin—and to celebrate renewed fellowship with God. Blood sacrifices were commanded: "No one is to appear before me empty-handed" (Exodus 23:15). But an Old Testament religious feast was fun too, not unlike a big honking Texas barbecue on the fourth of July. God likes fun.

Describe the joy you experienced in sacrifice.

It Is Finished

Read Genesis 22:1-14. Little Isaac, tied on a pile of kindling atop a mountain altar, was a symbol so rich in meaning that many people miss the layers. Not only did it foreshadow the cross, it was a sign to Abraham of what *not* to do. Human sacrifice was required by other gods, not Yahweh. Our souls recoil in horror at the idea of Abraham taking dagger in hand, of a child stabbed and roasted. Yes, Yahweh required blood for sin. But the old covenant took a balanced approach: just enough gore to convey the seriousness of sin, but no more. God didn't want Isaac's body; he wanted Abraham's heart.

PRAYER

Pause right now and talk with God about your heart
condition.

Your life—spilling over with gratitude and
love—is your celebration, a daily sacrifice kept alive
for praise and service until that final breath. What
about the sacrifices you made? Has your fellowship
with God deepened because of your service?

It's done: Jesus' once-for-all sacrifice. You've
been redeemed, body and soul. Think deeply about
what that means: holy and acceptable to the living
God! How should that affect the way you live in
the world?

Stuart Briscoe says, in *The Communicator's
Commentary: Romans*: "Believers have the unique
privilege and tension-filled opportunity to live in
the present 'evil age' as members of the age to come.

Therein lies the thrill of much Christian living."

Tension-filled. Great way to put it. Think back on the tension-filled moments of the past few weeks: the planning, training, fund-raising, paperwork, travel, the arguments, the good-byes. Which moments were the most anxious?

Would it have been a loftier thing—better for the kingdom—to withdraw from the world, to isolate, contemplate, and self-mutilate like the mystics of old?

Jesus isolated himself in the wilderness, but only for forty days. He went off to pray alone, but only overnight. He didn't hurt himself. The world beat him up.

You may still be a little beat up from your journey. Exhausted. Achy. Jet laggy. The result of your spiritual service. It was a reasonable, logical act of service—one that made sense and produced results.

Brutal Honesty

Take a hard, honest look back at how you've spent your life (because a person can hardly criticize medieval ascetics if he's been killing himself for years over nothing).

Now look ahead. If God should grant you "threescore years and ten" (Psalm 90:10, *KJV*), how many years do you have left? What could you do for him in a year? in five? How do you want to spend your time from here on?

Masochists need not apply for missions. There's genuine hard work to do. This is just an observation, but I believe Peter, Paul, Jeremiah, Ezekiel, Daniel, and Hosea would back me up on it: the things you suffer for Jesus should help people and build up the body of Christ, not form a dark red puddle on a stone step.

Reasonable ways to pour out your life are simple. You already know them: worship, plant a garden, talk about Jesus, listen to the grieving, earn a living, study the Bible, give generously, bless a child, pray for the lost, sing loudly in church, love your family, put money in the offering plate. Go about doing good. That will pretty much take up your whole threescore years and ten. Try not to deliberately hurt yourself in the process.

Some of us may have to let blood for God. Living for Jesus wholeheartedly might eventually kill you. Let's face it—*something's* gonna eventually kill you. Guaranteed.

No need to rush it with barbed-wire underwear.

FROM HERE TO
KINGDOM COME

Half of the 4 million people in my home state may be lost. A day's drive and I could reach them all. The fields are ripe for harvest right within a day's drive—or right down the street. What's the total population of your state? Even if 50 percent know Jesus as Lord and Savior, how many don't? How has this faraway mission trip changed your attitude toward people close to home?

John Dawson, in the *Worldwide Perspectives* curriculum, says, "It is impossible to love 'the lost.' You can't feel deeply for an abstraction or a concept. You would find it impossible to love deeply an unfamiliar individual portrayed in a photograph . . ." (That's why we toss those pictures from a new wallet or a picture frame and put in the face of someone we know: husband, wife, kids. And grandkids! Don't get me started.) ". . . let alone a nation or a race or something as vague as 'all lost people.'"

If you have pictures at hand from your mission trip, look at the faces of those you met. Isn't it funny how one can feel so close to another who is so far away?

Once you've been to a place, you can still smell it, hear it, taste it. The ability to do so is crucial when writing fiction. You must go to a place and fill the senses to write authentically.

Before traveling through Ireland, I saw many a pastoral scene in pictures, but it was nothing like 360 degrees of green in every shade imaginable—in late October! The pungent smell of a sheep pasture, the damp and spongy feel under my feet, a raven's silent sweep through the fog and over a castle wall. No European guidebook gives you that.

It's been a few days. Think back and fill your five senses again. Bring it home.

Who did you see? What did you hear? Who touched you? What smells in the air, what kinds of food or weather do you associate with that place?

Familiarity is vital to loving the lost.

Hallowed Be

In his article in *Worldwide Perspectives*, John Piper states, "Jesus' primary concern—the very first petition of the prayer he teaches—is that more and more people, and more and more peoples, come to hallow God's name. This is the reason the universe exists. Missions exists because this hallowing doesn't."

PRAYER

Before going further, stop and pray the Lord's Prayer (Matthew 6:9-13), pausing to meditate on each phrase. Think deeply on "hallowed be your name" and "your kingdom come."

Your Will Be Done

God's name Yahweh and the name of his Son Jesus are not hallowed, or holy, to most of the world. His will is not being done everywhere on earth. A few doors down, people are struggling and dying—no different from those who struggle and die a thousand miles away. It's the same all over the world.

What opportunities can you pray about, things you can do where God has you right now?

I took a close look at my own church for ideas. We're a small church of two hundred people. Not everyone in our little family is outwardly or heavenly focused. But in the past two years: Ed and Susan went short-term to Tijuana. Nan, Lynnette, and Charles went to Morocco. Bill and Emma occasionally go global with a senior travel club, spreading goodwill, handing out Bibles.

Planning another short-term trip may be what *you* need to be doing.

Locally, two of our men speak for the Gideons. Doris is the box lady; not that she lives in one, but at Christmas her house becomes an assembly line of toys and toiletries. Her volunteer staff gets four hundred Christmas boxes to children in Africa. Sue has a dynamite Wednesday program for neighborhood kids. Kelly and Robin have a puppet ministry. Tony and a dedicated team of volunteers run a TV ministry. Charles and Chink lead worship at the nursing home. A dozen or more assist with homeless ministry. Gail started making shawls for the sick and aged. Steve helps organize a yearly pig roast for the neighbors, as well as the town's fall festival. Others participate in the elementary school's readiness day and a children's fair. Many contribute to the local food pantry. Everyone contributes to missions and other Christian agencies.

Teens serve on worship and tech teams; once a year they do chores at a farm for the mentally disabled. The youth group has a yearly "30-hour famine" to raise money to fight hunger.

Numerous acts of kindness, hospital calls, free legal advice, and meals for the grieving go mostly unnoticed. No brag, just fact. We're an ordinary bride of Christ in an ordinary town.

Look at the ministries your church does. Ask around. Chances are you'll be stunned. At no time in world history is a church—even a small one—more equipped and able to change the world from home. Any possibilities surfacing for you?

Yours Is the Kingdom

At www.joshuaproject.net you can see the population of countries around the world, as well as the breakdown by people groups. There are over 300 million people and 314 people groups in the U.S. Those staggering numbers indicate an unlimited amount of home missions that could be done.

TRAVEL

How has your experience afar changed what you feel
about the needs nearby? What mission field is only a
one-tank trip away?

How far *is* it to kingdom come? From where I
sit it's two hundred and fifty miles—to Kingdom
Come State Park, Kentucky. The Magic Kingdom
is an eighteen-hour drive, the United Kingdom a
day's flight.

The kingdom of Heaven is right here.

ANYWHERE WITH JESUS

There was no projector screen for the missionary's slide presentation at the little country church. These were the olden days—the early '70s—before PowerPoint. The lady bringing a bed sheet to use as the screen had arrived late. As the song service proceeded, Larry, the lanky student preacher, climbed on a metal folding chair behind the song leader (you know where this is going) to hang the sheet.

He reached too far; the chair folded. Lanky Larry went flying as the congregation heartily sang, "Anywhere with Jesus I can safely go."

Mysterious Ways

God moves people in mysterious ways. He moved David from the pasture to the palace, Moses from the palace to the desert, Elijah from the desert to sudden infamy on Mt. Carmel, Jacob from here to there and everywhere, Paul from the high court of the Sanhedrin to the prison cell.

Think of a few more Bible characters; how and where did God move them?

God has moved you far away and brought you back. Did you feel the Lord's presence in a powerful way on the field, and now you're fighting back feelings of same old, same old? Coming home, you might go though a season of spiritual depression.

Spiritual depression is defined in a number of ways, but what I mean here is lingering grief over spiritual matters. It looks like situational depression because the root is the same: loss. Grief is a natural human response to loss. But if it settles in or becomes debilitating, it's depression.

One may feel a disconnect from loved ones after a mission trip. You may view your old, comfortable way of thinking as a thing of the past. And you might be right. Some short-termers deal with regret: *Why haven't I done this before? All that has needed to be done for the Lord, and here I have sat for years!*

Spiritual depression strikes deeply. You may, like Abraham, realize you must take your dearest attachments—the people and things that formerly defined you (job, home, family)—and lay them on the altar of the eternal. Going on ventures for God can radically shift your worldview.

Elijah and Jonah had suicidal thoughts. Moses was emotionally and physically overwhelmed. Paul despaired of his life, as did Jeremiah. God did not spare these and other spiritual giants from the abyss.

You've been faced with the suffering of others, and now that shallow saying that once seemed so rational—"God wants me to be happy"—is out the window.

If you're feeling low about the spiritual and physical condition of the people you left behind, if you're grieving over the loss of that place far away . . . or if you're glad it's over, and feeling a bit guilty for thinking it . . .

Express your thoughts.

Look over this list of causes of spiritual depression:

- **Negative attitudes.** Sadness or anger should motivate you forward to constructive change. If they lock in, crowding positive feelings out, you'll find yourself feeling bitter. Work through those feelings now.
- **Unrepented sin.** Look back at your trip. Feelings of guilt over wrongdoing—though uncomfortable—are good, if you use them to seek the Lord anew. Repent, take steps to change, let it go, and then move on.
- **Unexpected trials.** It's hard to realize that a loving God would put you through hardships when he has all power to rescue you. Did you expect blessings for your sacrifice and instead met with trouble? Trials refine the soul. Let them do their work.
- **Demonic attack.** Satan will manipulate natural emotions to push you toward the brink of the abyss. Resist him. Surround yourself with loving believers.

How Big Is God Anyhow?

Christians are taught that God is omnipotent. That said, let's be honest. Each of us has subconscious parameters on God's omnipotence, don't we? Of course we do. We spread our arms and say, "He's *this* big, bigger than anything." But we measure his bigness by our experiences with him, which—if we've led sheltered lives—are small. He has power over evil, we say, but the evil we have faced to this point may have been relatively small as well. Mostly, we may reason, we've been able to handle things ourselves, not requiring much from our Supreme Being.

This disparity between God's actual omnipotence and our estimation of him comes to crisis when evil looms larger than we ever imagined, when the beast rears one of its many ugly heads, one we haven't seen before. It's then that our concept of God and what he is able to do is overshadowed. Evil looks bigger than

God. The result: spiritual crisis. If that has that ever happened to you, jot down some of the details.

Imagine how the disciples felt when they thought that Jesus—the healer, the stiller of storms, the one who fed five thousand and raised the dead—had lost out to an enemy named Death. Live in their shoes for a moment through the ultimate spiritual crisis: how could Jesus conquer Death now that it had conquered him? The disciples knew he was the Son of God, but they'd also seen the horror of the cross. God's Messiah was . . . dead?

Evil loomed large on that Friday and Saturday. The disciples hid themselves away for fear of Death—and he was after *them* now.

And God left them there, hunkered down in shadows, in spiritual crisis.

If the sin and suffering you saw on mission has

you overwhelmed, wait on the Lord. Watch how he will reveal his majesty to meet the crisis. His almightiness will rise to the occasion, working in you and through you. If your widened world has become a scary place in the past weeks, concentrate on this Scripture of power: "I am the LORD, the God of all mankind. Is anything too hard for me?" (Jeremiah 32:27).

Take your doubts and fears to the Lord. Express creatively with poetry, song, or art on the blank pages of your journal. Don't be shy. He's heard it all before.

"He who began a good work in you will carry it on to completion" (Philippians 1:6). He is greater than you or I could ever, ever, ever imagine.

Sing all the verses of "Anywhere with Jesus." Write the lyrics in your journal as a testimony to his omnipotence and omnipresence.

MOUNTAINTOP
EXPERIENCES

Perhaps you're not feeling any of the dark emotions we discussed yesterday. The mission trip was one big blast of total fun? All mountaintop, no valley?

Mountaintop experiences are not all they're cracked up to be. I've been up a few mountains. You probably have too. I'll bet it wasn't all sunlight and roses. We're not talking air-conditioned RV to a "rustic" lodge with hot tubs and five-star dining. We're talking rough ascent.

Mountain climbers frequently fall to their deaths or have body parts frozen off. You get hungry up there on the heights. You pull muscles and get blisters. Sure the view is great—if the fog ever clears or the blizzard lets up or the bears don't attack.

On my first little mountain climb, my friend got whacked on the head with a stray boulder and nearly slipped over a precipice. My biggest mountain experience was to the summit of Mt.

Fuji: a dormant volcano and the epicenter of regular seismic rumblings. Elevation: 12,388 feet.

We drove halfway up the mountain, bought walking sticks, and started. The trail was sometimes rocky, more often ashy: two steps forward, one step back. The August morning had been muggy as we set out from the parking lot, though we were already above the clouds. At the summit, however, snow lay in crevasses; 60 mph winds whipped. We huddled in a "hotel," one of many stone huts along the way, which were built to be buried under snow most of the year. We sat around a fire in the hut like ill-equipped Sherpas—I had a light jacket and had eaten all my food hours ago. We drank tea, priced mountain-high. We heard tales of people getting blown off the mountain by sudden gusts.

My mountaintop experience at the summit hardly rivaled an Everest adventure . . . or the spiritual quests of Abraham, Moses, and Elijah.

Before going to the crater, I made a dash to the "squatty potty," as we Westerners call them: a dark, cold, uncomfortable outhouse with no seat, just a hole in the floor. My mountaintop meditations were interrupted by a rumbling sound; the outhouse began to tremble and shake.

Oh no, I thought. *Oh . . . no . . . !*

This was not my preferred way to die: in an outhouse on a volcano during an earthquake. Awaiting a humiliating death, the humor of the situation began to dawn. *This is a good one, Lord. A good one . . .*

Fortunately, the rumbling and shaking wasn't a sleeping volcano waking from its three-centuries-long nap. A bulldozer was grading off for another "hotel." I survived. But I never saw the crater for the clouds. The thin air, strong sun, and abrasive volcanic ash blasted a layer of skin off my face. My brother-in-law had marble-size blisters on his.

TRAVEL

A skin-care testimonial for future reference: For a few days after the climb, I kept my face moistened with water and Oil of Olay. I didn't blister. I've read similar testimonials. Keep sunburns and windburns cool and lightly moisturized. A bandanna to serve as a face mask would have helped too.

Not All They're Cracked Up to Be

Another potential bummer about mountaintop experiences: lots of work followed by big disappointment. I've been to the summit of three volcanoes and have yet to see a crater, due to the stinking sulfur and clouds. The views—if you can see them—are inspiring. But *National Geographic* magazines have award-winning photos of such places. Check out a copy at your local library for free and save on medical bills.

Abraham on the mountain thought he'd have to slaughter his own son (Genesis 22). He was grateful for the valley!

Moses on the mountain received the Ten Commandments the first time, and returned to commune with the Almighty . . . only to have his attention diverted to an orgy below: Israelites breaking most of the commandments they'd received (Exodus 19, 20, 32).

Elijah on the mountain escaped Jezebel's wrath, only to face blistering wind, earthquake, and fire before that final gentle whisper (1 Kings 18, 19).

Elijah couldn't stay on the mountain. He had to

confront false worship and a dearth of true believers. Moses and Abraham had herds of people to tend.

So do you.

CULTURE

Most world religions have their holy high places. But most have lost their specificity and have become simply sacred places of the one-mountain-fits-all variety. Mt. Shasta in California was a Native American holy mountain long ago. Now it's a site for the Buddhist/New Age Wesak festival. Mt. Kailash in Tibet is a holy mountain for both Buddhists and Hindus—though one wonders why Buddhists would revere the residence of the *Hindu* gods Shiva and Shakti. Pilgrimages to this mountain are taken by Jains as well and by non-religious adventurers.

There's Uluru/Ayers Rock in Australia, Croagh Patrick in Ireland, Katahdin in Maine, the four sacred mountains of the Navajos . . .

Holy mountains are a dime a dozen.

What inspires mountain worship? Long before Moses met God on Sinai, earth inhabitants attempted to reach God by building a man-made mountain: Babel. The Lord scattered them across the earth. They kept on trying: pyramids in Egypt, Mesoamerica, and little-known ones in China, Nubia, France, Peru, and Italy; earth mounds such as in Cahokia, Illinois.

Coming Down

Mountains symbolize strength and stability.

It was from the valley, however, that David said, "I lift up my eyes to the hills—where does my help come from? My help comes from the Lord, the Maker of heaven and earth" (Psalm 121:1, 2). The mountain maker, not the mountain, was his source of strength.

You can't stay on the mountain. Its purpose is to change your viewpoint. Was your experience a trial like Abraham's, an encounter like Moses', an escape like Elijah's? Or closer to a few scary minutes in a squatty potty?

God works with each of us differently, doesn't he?

Climbing Mt. Fuji took seven hours. Coming down took an hour, skiing through ashes. The next day I was in bed, tending to burns and pulled muscles. The pain went away. But I still have the walking stick, which was stamped at every station on the way up, including at the summit. I made it. I'll never throw that stick away.

It's exhilarating at the summit, but no one lives there. Mountaintops are about the ascent, the struggle, the companionship along the way, and the breathtaking view that you carry with you forever. If your mission trip was a mountaintop experience, awesome! You're in the descent now. The air gets warmer, more breathable. Your backpack of supplies is long gone.

This may be a good time to share with family members about *their* mountaintop experiences, over coffee and dessert. Perhaps you've never done this before. You'll learn about each other by sharing the highs.

RELIGION INCARNATE

This devo has more questions than answers.

Someone has said that culture is religion incarnate. The phrase keeps rolling around in my head. It's a catchy phrase and seems to make sense. Yet something doesn't set right, perhaps because those three words—*culture, religion,* and *incarnate*—have become so muddled in recent days.

Culture

Definition number one in my dictionary is: "the act of developing the intellectual and moral faculties, especially by education," as in "*cultivating* a better life." We who are older will remember a time when *culture* usually meant this very thing. Some folks had culture (mostly rich people and the British), and some folks didn't (people who owned spittoons and wore the same underwear for a month).

In today's jargon, however, definition five in the dictionary gets the most use: "the customary beliefs, social forms, and material traits of a racial, religious, or social group."

See the subtle shift, how the term *culture* has taken a step down, from cultivating a better life to simply how a people group lives—whatever that way may be?

We hear a lot about the importance of "celebrating one's culture" and "preserving the culture." Does this mean each group's habits and traditions are to be affirmed simply because they're . . . culture?

The time is coming—and is already here—when *preserving the culture* will mean "keep your Christianity and your Jesus out of my life." *Celebrating the culture* will mean—and already does mean—"However I want to live is worth celebrating" (morality and truth aside).

Most of what we call culture is morally neutral: food, housing, clothes, music, language. Some aspects of every society, though, stand in opposition to God's truth.

List a few aspects of the culture you left behind that were clearly not worth celebrating and were not developing a better life for the people. Then take a turn analyzing your own culture.

Religion

The word *religion* is also taking a bit of a beating. You may be surprised to hear good church people saying that religion is bad, even though the Bible clearly states that religion in its purest form is a good thing: "Religion that God our Father accepts as pure and faultless is this: to look after orphans and widows in their distress and to keep oneself from being polluted by the world" (James 1:27).

Real religion is caring for hurting people and living a life pleasing to God. What's not to like? Of course, by God's standards there *is* such a thing as false religion. But these days, to declare that someone's religion is "false" is not PC. Better to chat in terms of *spirituality*, or shift gears and be cool toward the whole idea of religion. Change the definition; then say that religion stinks.

This probably explains what we're hearing in Christian circles—you can't have missed it: "Christianity is not a religion; it's a relationship." Sounds good. But refer back to the verse in James. Real religion is *very* relational: caring for people, living a holy life with God. Religion and relationship are not at odds.

Whose definitions of *religion* and *relationship* are we believing?

What were your observations about religion and relationship on the mission field?

Incarnate

This is a tricky one, so pay attention.

Incarnation means "the embodiment of a deity or spirit in some earthly form." Jesus was the only deity incarnate, the only God in the flesh.

Perhaps you haven't heard the buzz yet, but there's talk about people "incarnating Christ" in the culture nowadays. Sounds good, but . . . wait. Is it possible for us to be the very physical representation of the Godhead?

True, *incarnate* has a lesser meaning: "the epitome of," as in "Estelle incarnates elegance." But in a religious context, incarnation always involves a god taking on flesh.

Believers should think critically about claiming to incarnate Christ.

Are we being too picky about terminology? I don't think so. The phrase *incarnate Christ* came out of twentieth century occult literature and is rooted in Hindu lore. Says the mythic Krishna: "Whenever righteousness declines and unrighteousness increases, I make myself a body; in every age I come back" (*Bhagavad Gita*, IV 7, 8). In this tradition of god becoming man, once is not enough. He needs to do it again and again through multiple incarnations—or reincarnations, to be precise.

Who is redefining the incarnation of the living God in our culture? Who transplanted this concept from occult literature into our conversation? See the ever-so-subtle shift away from Jesus Christ to his current "incarnation"?

In Jesus of Nazareth "all the fullness of the Deity [lived] in bodily form" (Colossians 2:9). It's done. I need only point to him with a thankful heart and say, "Would you look at that? God loved us so much he became a man to show us the way! Follow him!"

Look to John 1:1, 14 for an explanation of

incarnation: "In the beginning was the Word, and the Word was with God, and the Word was God. . . . The Word became flesh and made his dwelling among us. We have seen his glory, the glory of the One and Only."

While on mission, you saw the need to speak simply and clearly. It's as important at home. Mess with biblical words and you mess with the gospel. Ravi Zacharias is quoted as saying, "If you change the meaning of a word, then you are trying to change the meaning of the world" (www.evcforum .net). What does he mean by this?

I warned there'd be more questions than answers.

Culture Is Religion Incarnate

So there we have it: The statement "Culture is religion incarnate" can mean anything, or nothing. Culture is good and religion is bad? We can incarnate the incarnate God? See how words may be stripped of meaning right under our noses?

What did Jesus say about culture? I'm looking through all the red words in the book of Luke . . . and I'm not seeing *culture* anywhere. I am seeing *kingdom* a lot. It looks like Jesus gives less attention to the way people are doing things and more on how he—and we—can make things better now and for eternity. Culturally, Jesus was a Jew. Yet Romans, Samaritans, and Canaanites accepted his love heartily. Jesus mastered that whole in-the-world-but-not-of-the-world thing.

What did Jesus say about religion? Jesus doesn't use the word in his sermons, but he preached about caring for others and obeying God's Word. Sounds like James's definition.

What did Jesus say about incarnate? He said, "I am."

Jesus—not culture—was religion incarnate. Hallelujah!

Spread the word.

_____

_____

_____

_____

_____

_____

_____

_____

_____

_____

_____

_____

_____

_____

GLOBAL POSITIONING: THE EAST

Let's take one more quick trip around the world. If you've been tracking with the other journals in this series, we've looked at world religions, the global search for a messiah; we've had stories from the "three religious hemispheres," including arachnevangelism tales—stories of missionaries and giant spiders. (This just in: My daughter Andrea and her husband Tye returned from a mission trip to Mexico as I was writing this. While there, they went tarantula hunting. Yes. They took bottles of water and a video camera to an open field dotted with large holes. They poured water down the holes until they flushed out a tarantula and filmed it running across the field. Later that week, one of the workers woke up with an unidentified bite on his face and a swollen eye.)

The purpose of this global trek is to sample some amazing, creative, and diverse ways the Holy Spirit is working through people. Despite growing persecution, nothing is stopping the Lord and his servants. Not the 10/40 Window, not Communism, not false religions.

Today's devo and the next two are workbook devos. Underline, circle, and make notes in the margins. Get on the Internet and find Web sites. (Note: Mention of a mission org is not necessarily an endorsement, just informational to represent the variety of service opportunities available.)

We'll start in . . . the East.

Religion

Very generally speaking, Eastern religions believe that the universe goes through endless cycles of creation; that all souls reincarnate in an evolution toward union with the divine and finally nirvana, which means "extinguished"; that new revelations come from "God" through swamis and gurus; that all life is part of the divine; that no one religion is the only way.

Logistics

Teaching English as a second language is a common way to make yourself useful in Asia. It's also a great introduction to missions, because knowing the other language is not an essential prerequisite; you are there to speak English. You might sign up for two months or two years.

TRAVEL

Asia is a distant and expensive short-term trip from some parts of the U.S. If you go sometime in the future, plan to stay at least a month to maximize what you've spent on airfare.

Impossible

If you are challenged by impossible missions, listen to these two from India: Theeba and her husband minister to Stone Age tribal peoples who often bring demon-possessed children infested with lice into Theeba's home to show them a different life.

Sheila and her husband work in Bihar, a state in northern India referred to as the "graveyard of missions." Her friends ridiculed her for going (*Women of the 10/40 Window* brochure).

Person of Interest

Pandita Ramabai (1858–1922), the daughter of a Brahmin priest, came in contact with the Scriptures in India. She fully accepted Jesus after a trip to England where the differences between Hinduism and Christianity could be more clearly seen. Pandita spent her life serving others. During her last fifteen years, she translated the Bible into Mahrathi. According to Lorry Lutz (*Women as Risk-Takers for God*), Pandita was the only woman in history to completely translate the Bible. On her mission's Web site is the motto: A life totally committed to God has nothing to fear, nothing to lose, nothing to regret.

Has a particular verse stuck in your mind throughout the trip? How about a phrase that's become your team motto? Write it here, or make a decorative motto on your art page.

Music

Frank is using music to connect with people, one goal being to encourage indigenous people to write, perform, and record their own music. Audio/video specialists are needed to record and distribute music, a method of evangelism that can work even in restricted countries. Other possibilities include coffee houses, music camp, or a music exchange program with a sister city. Music is a universal language.

Cross Culture

One mission to China is using business-as-mission strategy. They're seeing Chinese companies become "kingdom communities." Do you have dreams of starting a business in China's booming economy?

Though located in Hong Kong, one established mission reaches Filipinos. There are more than one hundred thousand Filipinos living in Hong Kong. How could your passion for missions work in the global "churn" of people groups?

One Christian high school group went on a cross-cultural trip to Japan. It's a ton of work to plan, a project for those gifted in administration who want to inspire teens for missions.

Here's one for the Go Figure files: One woman in east Asia began witnessing to monks—in Buddhist temples. In some Asian countries monks are eager to speak English. They are living in monasteries partly to get an education and may serve for only a few months or years. Some are eager to talk about Christianity, especially about Jesus.

From Home

Want to do Asian missions from home? What about Web networking? Tap into mission networks of your country of choice. Offer to keep an exchange student. Give. In poorer countries such as Thailand, Laos, and India, even a few dollars go far.

Women in oppressive cultures make and sell crafts. How could you help? Find a way to sell their items at craft fairs or mission conventions.

Sri Lanka: A pastor started a church in 1997 where there were no Christians. That year Buddhist extremists broke both his hands. In 1998 they burned his house. In 1999 they interrupted the service and stabbed him.

That year seven hundred people were baptized.

In 2004, sixty-four of his family members died in the tsunami. He and his wife took in orphaned nieces and nephews. He cried to the Lord about his ministry: what could one man do? The pastor said that the Lord spoke to him: "I am coming soon. Go house to house." The pastor needed to reach five hundred thousand homes with the gospel! How was this possible? He printed up tracts with testimonies of healing, salvation, and deliverance from drugs and occultism. Volunteers have helped him hand out sixty thousand tracts to date.

Seven hundred more have come to know Jesus. Some of the Buddhist priests who persecuted him have come to the Lord, while others are pressuring the government to protect Buddhism. He requests prayers! (the *Southeast Outlook*).

PRAYER

Find a mission that touches your heart, and pray! You may not know until Heaven what effect your prayers had. But pray anyway.

CULTURE

Not all Buddhists are peaceful; the history of the East bears this out. Nor are all Muslims militant. Not all Americans wear cowboy hats either. Take care to avoid stereotypes, whichever hemisphere you're in.

GLOBAL POSITIONING: AFRICA AND THE MIDDLE EAST

This is the second of three workbook devos. Make notes. Get on the Internet and investigate opportunities.

"Abraham said to God, 'If only Ishmael might live under your blessing!'" (Genesis 17:18).

Though Isaac was to receive the special blessing of messianic lineage, Abraham prayed a heartfelt blessing for his firstborn, Ishmael.

Not Ready for Prime Time

What is going on among the children of Ishmael (the Arab Muslims)? And the whole Middle East for that matter? Things you won't see on the secular news.

"I see many, many Arabic-speaking people turning to Christ," said Nizar Shaheen, host of Light for the Nations, a Christian program seen throughout the Muslim world. It's happening in the Middle East, in Europe, Canada, and the U.S. Zakaria Boutros, an Egyptian priest and evangelist, concurs: "What's happening nowadays in the Muslim world has never happened before: young and old, educated and not educated, males and females, even those who are fanatic."

Samer Achmad Muhammed studied for years to become a sheik of the virulent Wahhabi sect of Islam. He hated the church until he heard the gospel. After that, he says, "I dedicated my life to Jesus Christ, Jesus forgave me for my sins" (www.cbn.com).

PRAYER

Did anyone on your trip do a similar about-face? Do *you* feel a need for a fresh turnaround, to start over, to set new goals? Have you thought of publicly rededicating your heart to Jesus? Pray about those changes.

Satellite television penetrates the world of Islam. While Christian broadcasting is fraught with controversy—and you may not care for some of the hairdos and music—gospel TV does get the Word to the unreached (and in many respects unreachable) Arab world. They see a side of America that's not all *Baywatch* and *South Park*.

CULTURE

Here's another for the Go Figure files: Garbage City, Egypt. Use Google or YouTube to get the appalling details. Desperately poor people live in a Cairo slum piled high with garbage, collecting and recycling the city's waste. The stench is eye-watering. Pigs and humans are fed from the same piles of refuse.

But many in Garbage City are believers. Close by, carved into a hillside, is the largest church in Egypt, a rustic sanctuary seating twenty thousand. And apparently some oppressed Christians in Cairo have moved to Garbage City just to be in community with other Christians.

Kareen just returned from a short-term trip there and reported that some folks even have TV reception, and they enjoy—get this—*The Simpsons*!

In places where even technology can't penetrate,

the Holy Spirit is apparently broadcasting good news. While Jesus made it clear that his physical coming will be global and unmistakable, dreams and visions about him are occurring among the children of Ishmael. Christine Darg, in *The Jesus Visions: Signs and Wonders in the Muslim World*, says that he is revealing "how He died on the cross, which Islam does not teach; how He was raised from the dead, which Islam also does not teach; and how He is the Son of God, risen in power."

TRAVEL

Africa and the Middle East are hotbeds of spiritual activity—and record-breaking temperatures. The hottest temp ever recorded on earth was 136 degrees Fahrenheit in 1922 in El Azizia, Libya (www.bigsiteofamazingfacts.com). The hottest average temperature—94 degrees—is in Dakol, Ethiopia (www.qna.live.com).

In May 2008, leaders at a meeting of the Protestant

Church of Algeria were in a heated debate: whether or not to obey the government. A law restricting non-Islamic worship was passed two years earlier. Half the churches have been closed. People have been arrested for possessing Bibles. Officials have made remarks equating Christian evangelism with terrorism.

The silver lining: Christian leaders believe the crackdown has resulted because of successful church plants and satellite TV ministries; the law exists because the church is growing. Some churches, though smaller because of persecution, are stronger. One leader says, "People you cannot rely on will step back."

What's the spiritual climate of your church? Is it growing? small but strong? fading?

In one Middle Eastern war zone, Christians are worse off since 9/11, according to PBS's *Frontline*. Many have escaped to neighboring countries where the situation is slightly better. Those who remain worship in small groups to avoid attack. American military personnel hesitate to overtly protect church buildings or meetings out of concern for creating more hostility.

On one battlefield (according to a woman whose nephew serves there), U.S. soldiers have been known to arrest native Christians and bring them in for questioning, but only on weekends. Why? Concerned Christian soldiers used this method to help persecuted believers meet safely for worship. It's spiritual warfare, with a twist.

PRAYER

Take some time right now to lift up in prayer the believing citizens and soldiers who live and work in war zones.

O Jerusalem!

Can you hear the pain in Jesus' voice as he stood over the city crying, "O Jerusalem, Jerusalem, you who kill the prophets and stone those sent to you, how often I have longed to gather your children together, as a hen gathers her chicks under her wings, but you were not willing!" (Luke 13:34).

Do Isaac's offspring still resist Jesus?

The year 2008 marks the sixtieth anniversary of the modern state of Israel. The messianic group Jews for Jesus polled Israelis about their opinions concerning Jesus. "What is the name of the Christian Messiah?" they asked. Only 8 percent said Y'shua (Hebrew for Jesus). Most who answered said Yeshu.

Since medieval times certain rabbis—believing Jesus to be a sorcerer—refused to speak the name Y'shua. They knocked off a letter to form Yeshu, which made an acronym for the Hebrew phrase, "May his name and memory be blotted out."

In one sense the curse has worked. The name Y'shua has been all but lost among Jesus' own people. And only 5 percent of those polled had ever heard that he rose from the dead.

The results are skewed, admits the polling company, because a record two-thirds of people questioned refused to participate when they heard the subject matter.

Undeterred, believers have stepped up bus ads and billboards with a Web site and phone numbers. They receive both hostile and curious calls.

Children of Abraham

The eyes of my messianic Jewish friend light up at the very mention of her long-time buddy, an Egyptian minister. They've been friends for years: a daughter of Isaac and a son of Ishmael. Worlds apart. One in Christ. Only because of him.

PRAYER

"If only Ishmael might live under your blessing!" prayed Abraham.

"O Jerusalem, Jerusalem," Jesus cried, ". . . how often I have longed to gather your children together."

Take a moment and globally position yourself to lift up everyone you know of the seed of Abraham—Ishmael or Isaac—that they might find peace and safety in Y'shua.

GLOBAL POSITIONING: THE WEST

We've thought of those other two hemispheres—the East, Africa and the Middle East—as largely unevangelized and unreached, wild and woolly. As we've seen though, the persecuted church is growing there.

In the West, however, it seems we're becoming dis-evangelized. We were once evangelized and evangelizers. Now the West is in a period of stagnation, even reversal.

But this isn't the whole picture.

Certain nations in the West are seeing growth and vitality. Brazil has one of the largest Christian populations in the world, with evangelical Christianity growing. Some countries have stabilized. Others with aging populations will not show the same growth among believers as those with high birthrates. The U.S. is still one of the top sending agencies. America is generous and resourceful.

We who are devoted to Jesus have better things to do than sit around listening to naysayers—especially our own brothers and sisters in Christ—who dis the church and take a tad too much pleasure in its decline in the West.

Ignore them and move on. You have big stuff to do. Westward ho!

PRAYER

These sections of the journal have provided prayer prompts. Prayer is key. However, C. T. Studd, missionary to China, India, and Africa, had harsh words for those whose prayer was not followed by action. He said, "When used as a substitute for obedience, it is nothing but a blatant hypocrisy, a despicable Pharisaism. . . . To your knees, man! And to your Bible! Decide at once! Don't hedge! Time flies! Cease your insults to God. Quit consulting flesh and blood. Stop your lame, lying, and cowardly excuses" (www.books.google.com).

Today, pray quickly and go *do* something for your Savior. Talk with him as you work.

The variety of opportunities for ministry in the West is amazing.

If You Build It . . .

One click on www.habitat.org and you can find the Habitat for Humanity affiliates in your area. The "theology of the hammer" is behind Habitat: anyone can show God's love by helping to provide housing for someone in need. A Bible is presented to the new owner.

Huck Finnin' It

Didn't you envy Huck floating down the river on his exciting adventures? No doubt Mark Twain romanticized river life. But if you're Huck Finnin' it for God, the harsh realities of a life afloat are worth it. Rivers of the World (www.gowithrow.com) aims to travel up remote river basins and help people in forgotten parts of the world. Much of their work is in Central and South America.

It's a Jungle Out There

And it's a mountain and a valley and a plain and a lonely village out there where 193 million people don't have "adequate Scripture" in their own language (www.wycliffefoundation.org). Wycliffe,

Pioneer Bible Translators, and New Tribes Mission are three major groups whose purpose is to translate God's Word and teach literacy to get the gospel out there.

Just as unreached peoples of the West need God's Word, the Hispanic world in the West needs solid biblical literature in their language. So Jon and Kathy Underwood began La Palabra de Cristo, a mission to translate and publish tried-and-true English books into Spanish. They license the product with the author, raise money for expenses, hire translators and proofreaders, and secure the printing. Then the hard part: marketing.

If *you* can't travel worldwide, books *can*. Some branch of publishing could become your mission.

CULTURE

If you are close to a computer, watch the video "Changed" at www.ntm.org/video. Understand that God is working everywhere. He desires to commune with every single person from every tribe, tongue, and nation. Where do you want to join him?

To Europe . . . and Beyond!

Lyndee is ministering in Norway, but her flight paths from there look like the maps you see in airline magazines, with lines arcing from a central point to all over creation. From her base in Skein, she has worked short-term in Europe, Asia, and Africa. Lyndee is in one respect a full-time short-termer. This kind of ministry requires great adaptability.

Repositioned

For decades we Americans have seen the U.S. as the primary sending country—and rightly so. It's time to reposition ourselves globally, to view God's work as expanding from many points around the world. Resist the temptation of resentment or jealousy, feelings inspired by the evil one. Share in the adventure from wherever you live.

PRAYER

C. T. Studd also said, "Christ does not want nibblers of the possible, but grabbers of the impossible" (www. worldofquotes.com). Today, ask God to give you an impossible task so he may show his glory through you.

We Ain't Out of the Woods Yet

Persecution is found mostly in the 10/40 Window: the Middle East and Asia. But there are dark places on the map in the western hemisphere as well. Voice of the Martyrs (VOM) reports one hot spot in Mexico, in the southern state of Chiapas. Church buildings have been destroyed, property seized, believers threatened, jailed, or killed by traditionalist Catholics with Mayan/animist beliefs who see the evangelical church as a threat (www.cbn.com).

Another hot spot: Cuba is still under a Communist regime at this writing.

Colombia is also on the VOM prayer map. The recent rescue of hostages from FARC (Revolutionary Armed Forces of Colombia) made headlines. The infiltration was hailed as a work of genius.

In spiritual warfare, Maria, a pastor's wife, goes unarmed into Colombian areas heavily controlled by the same terrorist organization. Since FARC doesn't expect a woman to be preaching the gospel, she's been able to go where very few people dare, giving Bibles to guerrillas. Some are coming to know Jesus (www.persecutionblog.com).

Pure genius.

The civilized West is in many places still the wild, wild West.

Think of a wild place near you where ministry requires uncommon courage. What can you do about it?

ARE WE THERE YET?

Good news! We Americans are not the world's most obnoxious Western tourists!

According to www.time.com the French are at the bottom of the Western barrel at number nineteen. Overall, the Chinese placed dead last in twenty-first place, with India's travelers at twentieth.

The survey was based on people's willingness to speak the native language, spend money, and sample local cuisine (it's kind of pathetic when a traveler ventures to Buenos Aries or Budapest and lives off Big Macs). Also evaluated: cleanliness, politeness, and elegance.

The best travelers? The Japanese for their quiet, tidy ways. Next in line were Germans, Brits, and Canadians. Italians were voted best dressed.

Overall, Americans came in at number eleven, in a tie with the Thais. A pleasant surprise: U.S. citizens topped the list for trying to speak local languages.

If you worked through the second journal in this series, *Challenged*, you'll remember reading that on foreign soil your every move is watched. It's true at home too, and ever more so in an environment increasingly hostile to Christians.

TRAVEL

We're God's reps everywhere. I encourage you to stay in "mission mode" in habit and decorum on a daily basis, to live as a changed person—changed not on the surface by a mission trip but from within by the work of the Spirit of God.

We may never attain Japanese refinement or European fashion, but we can scrape ourselves off the bottom of the tourist barrel for now. If you've had anything to do with this reversal of the "ugly American" reputation in recent years, kudos to you—and keep it up. We're getting there!

What are your thoughts about how you might present a better image of America to the world? How might you present a more accurate image of Christ?

Spreading the Word

Where is the world heading?

With regard to people groups: New Tribes Mission states that twenty-five hundred of the world's sixty-five hundred people groups are still unreached (www.ntm.org). Seems like a lot, but remember that many of those groups are relatively small. Still, we're a long way from finished with the Great Commission.

According to www.world-science.net, one language dies out about every two weeks. Cultural anthropologists would say that's a bad thing. Theologians would probably bicker amongst themselves; is this good for evangelism or a return to a one-language, tower-of-Babel rebellion?

However you look at it, we're not there yet.

With regard to the information highway: The Joshua Project and others are collecting detailed data to help us understand the world's spiritual condition and needs. This is a fantastic resource when researching a particular field. On the down side, those against faith in Jesus see such efforts as a large-scale intelligence operation bent on ruling the world.

Are You "There" Yet?

Where do you want to be? Do you want to go back to your recent field? This would be a hard pill to swallow, but they may not want you back. They may not need your skills; they may not like your personality. The missionary would probably be the last to tell you if he thought you were lazy, arrogant, or difficult.

If you'd like to return to this same mission, let the team leader and/or missionary know it; then leave the inviting to them.

Working with missionaries is a deeply personal relationship. They tend to function best in small, focused, interdependent communities. On-site staff are chosen carefully and with prayer. Don't invite yourself or assume intimacy where none may exist.

OK, enough browbeating. If you sincerely want to

serve your mission, you can certainly help, but in a way the missionary requests.

PRAYER
Take your desires for service to the Lord.

Who'll Be a Witness?

The word *missionary* is not in the Bible. The word *witness*, however, is found twelve times in the Acts of the Apostles. Notice it's not called the Good Ideas of the Apostles or the Big Dreams of the Apostles. Witnesses *act*: going, telling, doing. What specific things did the apostles do in the first century to witness? Skim through Acts to find out.

Jesus said, "You will be my witnesses in Jerusalem, and in all Judea and Samaria, and to the ends of the earth" (Acts 1:8). What an awesome call for us all! What a challenge! And how those words change our perspective on life.

The disciples were eyewitnesses; they had seen.

They were earwitnesses; they had heard.

They were soul witnesses: "We are witnesses of these things, and *so is the Holy Spirit*, whom God has given to those who obey him" (Acts 5:32, emphasis added).

The Spirit witnesses *to* you and *through* you.

When a believer for Jesus goes far, he's called a missionary. When he stays home he's called a witness, a servant, or minister. But it's the same thing.

Which is scarier—witnessing at home or far away? Why?

Peter said, "Dear friends, I urge you, as aliens and strangers in the world, to abstain from sinful desires, which war against your soul. Live such good lives among the pagans that, though they accuse you of doing wrong, they may see your good deeds and glorify God on the day he visits us" (1 Peter 2:11, 12; see also Philippians 3:20; Hebrews 11:13).

Now that you're home, are you looking around for a mission field, a witness stand?

You're there.

LIVING AMONG PAGANS

You've been around the world—on paper at least. See if you know where these religious practices are taking place:

- prayers to the Greek Earth Mother Goddess
- Buddhist mantras for healing and unity
- clay images of Asherah, goddess of the Canaanites
- witchcraft

If you answered "American churches" to all of the above, you'd be right.

No kidding. And we're not talking those weird fringe churches with names such as Tabernacle of the Golden Dawn or The Church of Universal United Unity. We're talking Methodist, Lutheran, Presbyterian, Baptist . . . To learn more, google from that list, or start with the article "Heresy in High Places" on www.crossroad.to.

Half of the top ten most atheistic countries are

in the West, including: Germany, France, the U.S., Britain, and Canada (www.adherents.com).

And here's a chilling post from a blog: "If [Buddhist teaching] could be taught in the Seminaries it might start to impact the various preachers 10 or 20 years down the road. This is the angle I'm working. If the preachers are inwardly 'Buddhists' in their hearts—then you don't need to beat your head against the wall dealing with ignorant congregants" (www.fraughtwithperil.com).

Ignorant congregants. Ouch. That's us he's talking about!

Why is this happening in the U.S.? Is it because Christianity is too demanding compared to New Age self-realization? Have we taken our eyes off Jesus and turned our attention elsewhere? Before pointing fingers, ask yourself, "What have I done—or not done—to lift up Jesus in my homeland? What idols have I taken in?"

"'Has a nation ever changed its gods? (Yet they are not gods at all.) But my people have exchanged their Glory for worthless idols. Be appalled at this, O heavens, and shudder with great horror,' declares the LORD" (Jeremiah 2:11, 12).

CULTURE

Now that you're home, reality may be slowly sinking in that your own society needs an overhaul. Maybe the place where you live is a little more "exotic" than you realized.

I found varying stats, but roughly between thirty-five hundred and four thousand churches close every year. To keep pace with population, we need to keep all those open and add at least a thousand more!

No need to be overwhelmed. The gospel is the work of the Almighty. We join him, letting him use us as he sees fit. Our freedoms, our faith, and our prosperity as a nation were hard won, but we didn't get this far alone. He's with us. Take heart and walk in his steps.

Changing your world equals spiritual warfare: you repent of the past, get into the Word, listen for the Spirit. You care for your fellow warriors and love your enemies, because your battle is not against them. You put on the armor of God, which is putting on Christ, so that when the day of evil comes, you can stand.

You can change the world. Jesus did it with twelve followers—fully loaded with the Spirit—and he can do it with us.

Homebound and Penniless?

You can still change the world. Pray. I have a map of the world in my office with tabs stuck on various countries where I know people. Whenever I feel boxed in and ineffective, I look at my map and pray. Like a backyard stargazer, one gets a feeling of quiet awe looking at the world, knowing God is above all and over all, that he has ordained my meager words to have eternal effect. Prayer is the lifeblood of the gospel!

World mission orgs send e-mail and printed updates from around the world to keep us informed.

This one came from the International Mission Board after the Myanmar cyclone disaster:

> Our personnel are supporting the nationals but are not allowed to go out themselves (foreigners cannot minister to those in need). Believers . . . are exhausted and sometimes feel very alone. Many of them must go through places flooded with water and dead bodies, to reach the survivors. The brothers and sisters you will write to are . . . feeding, doctoring, saving, loving, transporting these victims. They are completely exhausted and have no encouraging words left. They know they are not alone, but they feel alone. . . . To actually hear from you would be exponentially more encouraging. As they come back in to replenish supplies I would like to line their meeting room walls with real words of encouragement that come from real people who are praying for them.

Notes from home are gold to missionaries. If you're truly penniless, no prob! E-mail is free; use a home computer or the local library. Or get two other people to partner with you in snail mail: one buys the cards, you write them, a third stamps and mails.

Come Together

With minimum expense you and your church can mentor children. Or you can collect supplies, Bibles, or clothes to send overseas. Make a list of ministries your church participates in.

Ready for a maximum investment? Adopt an orphan, or take in one of the eighty thousand refugees heading from Myanmar (www.rd.com).

Beloved of God, if we never ever set foot outside our neighborhoods again, we'll continue to have global work cut out for us.

America is still the land of the free and the home of the brave. But the days of the cushy Christian—if they ever existed—are over.

Remember God's message delivered by Jeremiah: "If you really change your ways . . . then I will let you live in this place, in the land I gave your forefathers" (Jeremiah 7:5-7).

THE J WORD

I like Oprah. So it was unsettling to watch her create a "world's largest classroom" and teach theology in which "The Universe" is what you believe it to be, and this big U is just crazy about giving U whatever U want.

In a related televised question-and-answer segment, one woman asked Oprah, "What about Jesus?"

And Oprah—who hardly ever snaps at anyone—practically snapped back, "What *about* Jesus?!" (www.jesus-is-savior.com).

Jesus is always the problem.

John Warwick Montgomery says (in cheeky fashion), "The earliest records we have of the life and ministry of Jesus give the overwhelming impression that this man went around not so much 'doing good' but making a decided nuisance of Himself" (*History and Christianity*).

Read through one of the Gospels and see for yourself. Jesus was stern with his followers, nailed the Pharisees time and again, worried his family, gave attention to the dregs of society, wrecked perfectly good funerals, and gave Satan fits. He threw furniture, called names, pronounced curses, issued cryptic warnings, and used dreadful terms like "weeping and gnashing of teeth" and "lake of fire."

If you're a pagan or a cushy Christian, Jesus is a problem.

God's OK, but Jesus . . .

Most societies don't mind if you talk about God or gods. But just say the name Jesus in any number of places around the world, and prepare to duck. Hand out bottles of water and you're fine. Hand out bottles of water in Jesus' name—daring to say that name—and you might get a few expletives hurled back at you. Otherwise nice people curl a lip; eyes glaze over at the mention of his name.

What's been your experience when talking about Jesus in the States? What kinds of responses have you encountered?

Before further risking life and limb, know which Jesus you're representing.

Deepak Chopra wrote a new book, *The Third Jesus*, which is doing quite well in bookstores. Apparently the first Jesus—the one we read about in the Bible—is so lost in legend that we can't know him. The second Jesus—also fiction—was invented and evolved over centuries by a power-hungry church hierarchy wanting to control people.

But the third Jesus (the "real" one) taught Eastern mysticism: that there is no sin, that his salvation is nothing unique, and that his second coming will actually be a shift in our cosmic consciousness—the divinity within.

Regarding the first Jesus, F. F. Bruce said, "The earliest preachers of the gospel knew the value of . . . firsthand testimony, and appealed to it time and again. 'We are witnesses of these things,' was their constant and confident assertion. . . . The early Christians were careful to distinguish between the sayings of Jesus and their own inferences or judgments. . . . The disciples could not afford to risk inaccuracies (not to speak of willful manipulation of the facts)" (*The New Testament Documents: Are They Reliable?*).

Jesus' followers said, "We are witnesses of these things" (Acts 5:32) but also, ". . . as you yourselves know" (Acts 2:22).

What now is your firsthand testimony of Jesus?

Who Is He?

Descartes said, "I think, therefore I am."

Jesus said, "Before Abraham was born, I am" (John 8:58). He asked, "Whom do men say that I, the Son of man, am?" (Matthew 16:13, *KJV*).

"Who do you say that I am?" he still asks today. "What do you think of Christ? Whose son is he?"

PRAYER

Spend some time today telling Jesus what you think of him.

It's not who *we* are, but who *he* is that makes the difference. Who was Jesus to the culture you just left? An unknown? A myth? A great teacher? An embodiment of Christ consciousness? One of many gods to choose from? Was he Yeshu—he who shall not be named? Or was he Y'shua—salvation?

CULTURE

There is one Jesus, but he reveals himself to people from their point of need. In tribal cultures where the demonic is very real, believers see Jesus as a warrior, his name and Word as a weapon. In Eastern cultures where religion is based on ancient myth, seekers are often struck with the historicity of Jesus and of his Word. One young Japanese woman thought Jesus was a mythic Hercules-type character until she realized that the entire world reckons time—BC and AD—by Jesus' life. She decided this man of history was worth investigating.

Have you read the Bible all the way through? Look for Jesus on every page, from Genesis to Revelation. The God of the Old Testament? That's Jesus: creative, generous, patient, stern, powerful, destructive, mysterious, loving. In the New Testament he appears on the scene as an innocent baby, then a determined youth, and finally a purposeful adult: creative, generous, patient, stern, powerful, destructive, mysterious, loving.

It's Jesus who calls, challenges, and changes you; who lifts you from the depths to more than you can be; who himself became the lowest of the low; whose name—Y'shua, salvation—is above every name in Heaven and on earth.

Don't you just love him? Tell him so, here, in your own words. Solidify what you believe about him based on Paul's strong words in 2 Corinthians 11:4 and Galatians 1:6-10.

You, the journaling believer—or anyone who finds this book in the event it's lost—need to learn about Jesus for yourself, through the Word of God and prayer. Start with the book of John. Or start at the beginning, in Genesis. Ask God to reveal himself to you. He promises, "You will seek me and find me when you seek me with all your heart" (Jeremiah 29:13).

"The LORD searches every heart and understands every motive behind the thoughts. If you seek him, he will be found by you; but if you forsake him, he will reject you forever" (1 Chronicles 28:9).

"Whoever is thirsty, let him come; and whoever wishes, let him take the free gift of the water of life" (Revelation 22:17).

_____

_____

_____

_____

_____

_____

_____

_____

_____

_____

_____

_____

_____

_____

HARD TO REACH

I remember Russ as a wiry, energetic, fifty-year-old rich guy. He loved rebuilding cars and had a four-bay garage for that purpose. He was grainy-voiced and blunt, a no-nonsense doctor who explained why he'd chosen to be an anesthesiologist: "I put sick people to sleep so I won't have to listen to them whine."

He was a staunch advocate for neighborhood evangelism. One tale circulated about his unique method: Tired of knocking on door after door of an apartment complex and giving the same invitation over and over, he changed his strategy. He knocked on all the doors in one fell swoop, waited until the residents answered, then announced, "OK, I'm only going to say this once . . ."

He had a mischievous smile and a dry sense of humor. His wonderful wife, Jane, is as bubbly and warm as he was curmudgeon-like. A great pair. His boys were in our youth group, so the Summays hosted parties in their enormous rec room.

The chapel at Southeast Christian Church was

packed at Russ Summay's memorial service on March 6, 2008. No surprise there. But countless in absentia friends from all over the world were grieving too.

Missions!?

I didn't see the missionary side of Russ in the five years I worked with him. When we wanted to take a youth mission trip to Japan—in 1980 when short-term, long-distance youth missions were a rarity—Russ was blunt: "Why do you want to go there? They're the enemy." He may have been yanking our chains or testing our mettle. I wasn't sure. Russ was all about reaching the neighborhood. But once the trip was decided, he wholeheartedly supported it.

Years later, when asked to join the missions ministry, he hesitated. But once convinced, he became as forceful in recruiting short-termers as he was at apartment evangelism. Tina Bruner, missions ministry team leader at Southeast, said, "He believed in those who seemed unlikely, even unwilling . . . and he pushed us as a church toward people and places that seemed the hardest to reach."

The Final Product

Perhaps Russ's talent for missions reflected his expertise with rebuilding cars, reaching into those hard places. Ignoring the discomfort, prying stubborn nuts and bolts, he'd transform what looked like a heap of junk into a spotless, spiffy collector's model. Russ could envision the final product.

Russ's personality and gifts didn't change, but his focus intensified and expanded. From middle age till his death, Russ went to countries that were like the engine parts in a foreign sports car—hard to reach:

- East: Japan, India, Philippines
- Africa and Middle East: Ivory Coast, Eritrea, Afghanistan, Kenya, Ethiopia
- West: Cuba, France, Austria, Bosnia, Romania

Ruth Schenk, editor of the *Southeast Outlook*, devoted a full-page tribute to Russ Summay, including photos from Afghanistan, where he and Jane served during the Taliban rule.

Their elegant house, once a hangout for youth

parties, became a "hotel for missions." When he was too ill from cancer to travel, he'd show up at the mission office to do chores.

At his funeral the lines were an hour long. Flags from thirteen countries stood sentry on the platform.

We Shall All Be . . .

It's never too late to change—not necessarily who you are, but what you do, how much you do it, and where. As you work your way through the devos, prayers, and journal pages, is the Spirit settling you back into home ministries or leading you in another direction? What ideas are you tinkering with?

Change is hard. Obstacles loom. Are you in debt, running out of resources, getting old, battling disease, out of time? So's the world. Jesus told us it would be this way.

The psalmist, in a prophetic passage, said, "In the beginning you laid the foundations of the earth, and the heavens are the work of your hands. They will perish, but you remain; they will all wear out like a garment. Like clothing you will change them and they will be discarded. But you remain the same, and your years will never end. The children of your servants will live in your presence; their descendants will be established before you" (Psalm 102:25-28).

Russ's friends wondered how many people from every corner of the world would be in Heaven because of his crusty, nuts-and-bolts influence.

Brace yourself for a hard question, one that we all must ask ourselves: Who will be in Heaven to thank *you*?

The space above may be emptier than you'd like.

PRAYER

If that is true for you, talk to God about your desire to impact others with the message of Jesus.

Beloved of God, it's not too late to change, never too late to begin. Jesus told the story of the eleventh-hour laborers in Matthew 20. Whether you're a new believer, a late bloomer, or a lifelong servant, you've been called to the vineyard and challenged to bring in the harvest until quitting time—11:59:59 PM on the last day.

Change is inevitable. Change is hard. Change is good.

"I declare to you, brothers, that flesh and blood cannot inherit the kingdom of God, nor does the perishable inherit the imperishable. Listen, I tell you a mystery: We will not all sleep, but we will all be changed—in a flash, in the twinkling of an eye, at the last trumpet. For the trumpet will sound, the dead will be raised imperishable, and we will be changed" (1 Corinthians 15:50-52).

ABOUT THE AUTHOR

Lena Wood has a lifelong history of missions and writing. She has been on mission trips to Japan five times, has been involved in homeless ministry and children's ministry at her church in Kentucky, and maintains contact and prayer support for missionaries all over the world. A former editor at Standard Publishing, she has written articles, skits, songs, programs, and curriculum, as well as the seven-book youth fiction series Elijah Creek & The Armor of God (www.standardpub.com). Lena is an artist, a worship leader, and the mother of two grown daughters, Arian and Andrea.

www.lenawood.com